There Are No Polar Bears Down There

Written and Illustrated by Trish Hart

Down in Antarctica there are penguins,

seals,

and albatrosses . . .

but there are no polar bears down there.

Down in Antarctica there are whales,

dolphins,

and snow petrels . . .

but there are no polar bears down there.

So where are all the polar bears?
Up in the Arctic, that's where.